THE
LITTLE
NOODLE
COOKBOOK

THE
LITTLE
NOODLE
COOKBOOK

BY PATRICIA STAPLEY

ILLUSTRATIONS BY JENNIE OPPENHEIMER

CROWN PUBLISHERS, INC.
NEW YORK

For Chuck

I wish to thank the following people for their help and support: Aaron Stapley, Norma Daugherty, Jill Benson, Christine Carswell, Esther Mitgang, Rita Aero, Judith Maas, and Howard Rheingold.

Compilation copyright © 1993 by Fly Productions
Text copyright © 1993 by Patricia Stapley
Illustrations copyright © 1993 by Jennie Oppenheimer

Published by Crown Publishers, Inc., 201 East 50th Street, New York, New York 10022.
Member of the Crown Publishing Group.

CROWN is a trademark of Crown Publishers, Inc.

Manufactured in Hong Kong

Library of Congress Cataloging-in-Publication Data
Stapley, Patricia
The little noodle cookbook / by Patricia Stapley; illustrations by Jennie Oppenheimer.—1st ed.
p. cm.
Includes index.
1. Cookery (Pasta) I. Title
TX809.M17S72   1993
641.8'22—dc20   92-15457
CIP

ISBN 0-517-58788-2

1   3   5   7   9   10   8   6   4   2

FIRST EDITION

CONTENTS

INTRODUCTION

Simple to prepare, simply delicious, and easy on the pocketbook, the ubiquitous noodle is versatile and various. Noodles are perfectly suited to the inventive cook who enjoys preparing mouthwatering meals using an international array of spices and herbs.

Who "invented" the noodle — the Italians or the Chinese? Certainly both cuisines have staked a legitimate claim. Most Westerners know and adore Italian dried pasta. The best is made by mixing water with the ground inner grain of hard durum wheat called durum semolina. High in gluten, durum flour produces resilient noodles that are perfect when served al dente (cooked tender on the outside, but pleasingly firm on the inside).

Throughout Asia, and particularly in China, delicious noodles are made from mung beans, rice, whole-wheat, or buckwheat flours. The Asian-style egg, whole-wheat, or buckwheat noodles are cooked in the same way as Italian-style pasta is, by boiling in water or stock until al dente. Noodles made from mung beans are commonly called cellophane noodles. Like Asian rice noodles, cellophane noodles cook beautifully soft by soaking in hot or cold water to rehydrate.

Each recipe gives the cooking time for the specific noodle you will be preparing. Refer to "The Little Noodle I.D. Chart" (see the following page) for illustrations of the noodles you will be cooking.

All but three of the recipes in *The Little Noodle Cookbook* call for dried noodles. Dried noodles contain no cholesterol, have more protein and vitamins, and usually less fat than the fresh and they keep for years in the cupboard. Fresh pasta, made of eggs and all-purpose flour, has a richer taste and a

The Little Noodle I.D. Chart

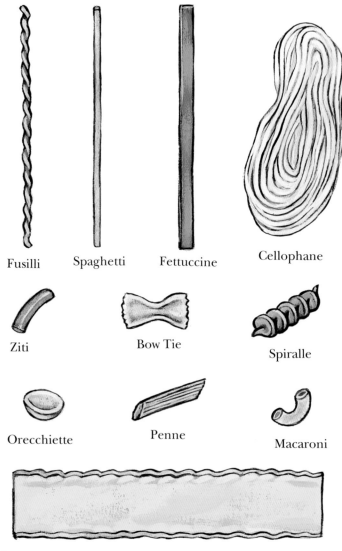

Fusilli   Spaghetti   Fettuccine   Cellophane

Ziti   Bow Tie   Spiralle

Orecchiette   Penne   Macaroni

Lasagne

lighter texture than the dried. Generally it freezes well, but will keep for only a few days in the refrigerator. Fresh Asian-style noodles are harder to come by. Many supermarkets carry fresh Italian pastas, but fresh Asian noodles are usually only available in specialty or gourmet stores.

If you choose to substitute fresh noodles in a recipe that calls for a dried variety, you must drastically reduce the cooking time. For instance, thick pastas made of egg and flour like tagliatelle or *lo mein* will cook al dente in about sixty seconds. The flat-shaped linguine takes no more than forty seconds. And, the fresh cellophane noodles can be served at room temperature without cooking or plunged into boiling water or stock for about twenty seconds to serve hot.

The general cooking technique, however, is the same for every kind of dried wheat-flour noodle. To prepare sixteen ounces of pasta, bring five quarts of water to a rapid boil. Use the largest pot you have. Add the noodles, stirring them once or twice for the first minute or two of cooking time to keep them separated. I like my pasta cooked al dente, soft on the outside, but slightly chewy on the inside. If al dente is not to your liking, cook a minute or two longer, and the pasta will have an even softness outside to inside.

Every recipe is followed by the fiber, cholesterol, and fat count for each serving. Most of the dishes have a "Lean Noodle Tip" in case you want to modify the recipes for diets restricted in saturated fats or cholesterol — but not in flavor.

Ideal for improvising on a moment's notice, the seventeen main-course dishes in *The Little Noodle Cookbook* offer a noodles-eye view of glorious country cooking the world over.

Parisian Bow Ties Dressed Wild in Mushrooms

Luscious, lavish, and delicious, this gorgeous dish is a chorus of rich flavors — woodsy wild mushrooms, a whisper of sweet aperitif, and a silken drop of cream make Parisian Bow Ties a pièce de résistance. Bring the evening to a triumphant conclusion with a flute of champagne, a tartare of smoked salmon, and a sorbet of wild strawberries.

Makes Four Servings

1/2 cup white Lillet wine
1/4 cup mixture of dried mushrooms: cèpes, morels, and chanterelles, rinsed thoroughly
3 tablespoons olive oil
2 tablespoons minced shallots
1 tablespoon minced garlic
4 large fresh chanterelle mushrooms, cleaned and thinly sliced
8 medium fresh cultivated mushrooms, cleaned and thinly sliced
salt and freshly ground black pepper to taste
1/2 cup beef or vegetable stock
3 tablespoons heavy cream
16 ounces bow tie noodles
1 teaspoon minced thyme, or 1/4 teaspoon dried

1 teaspoon minced chervil, or 1/4 teaspoon dried
1 teaspoon minced sage, or 1/4 teaspoon dried
2 tablespoons chopped parsley

In a small saucepan, bring the Lillet to a boil. Remove the pan from the heat, add the dried mushrooms, and set aside to rehydrate.

In a large pot, bring five quarts of water to a boil.

Heat the oil in a large skillet. Add the shallots and the garlic. Sauté over medium-low temperature for two minutes. Add the fresh chanterelles and cultivated mushrooms and cook for five minutes.

Drain the rehydrated mushrooms. Reserve the Lillet. Coarsely chop the mushrooms and add them to the skillet. Cook for one minute. Add the Lillet. Season with salt and pepper to taste. Cook for five minutes, or until the Lillet has been reduced by about half. Add the stock. Bring it to a boil. Stir in the cream and continue to cook, stirring occasionally for about ten minutes.

Add the bow tie noodles to the pot of boiling water and cook until al dente, eight to ten minutes. Drain, and transfer to a warmed ceramic serving bowl.

Remove the skillet from the heat. Add the thyme, chervil, sage, and parsley. Stir to combine well. Dress the Parisian Bow Ties with the sauce. Serve immediately.

Set your table with panache — crystal goblets, silver service, and gleaming white china. *Bon appétit!*

Lean Noodle Tip: Substitute a well-flavored vegetable stock for the beef stock.

Each Lean Noodle serving contains:
- FIBER: 1.7 GRAMS • CHOLESTEROL: 15.8 MILLIGRAMS
- FAT: 16.4 GRAMS

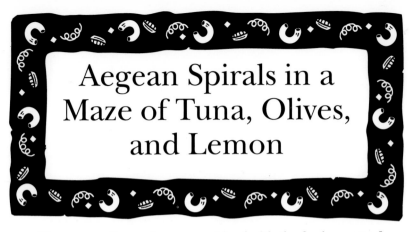

Aegean Spirals in a Maze of Tuna, Olives, and Lemon

The aroma of tangy lemon combined with the fresh scents of a sea breeze will tease your palate for this savory sensation. Aegean Spirals takes hardly any time to cook, so it's an ideal dish for a lazy summer's evening after a day at the beach. Dally over some stuffed grape leaves and sip a chilled glass of retsina to accompany this zesty offering.

Makes Four Servings

3 small lemons
16 ounces spiralle noodles
3 tablespoons virgin olive oil
2 tablespoons capers
12 kalamata olives, pitted and coarsely chopped
3 cloves garlic, peeled and finely chopped
7 ounces water-packed chunk tuna, drained
2 tablespoons chopped fresh parsley
salt and freshly ground black pepper to taste

In a large pot, bring five quarts of water to a boil.

Cut the ends off all the lemons, peel them, and carefully remove the bitter white pith. Slice one lemon into thin rounds and set aside for garnish. Cut the other two lemons into round slices and then quarter into wedges. Set aside.

Pour the spiralle noodles into the rapidly boiling water

and cook until al dente, about eight minutes. Remove from the water, drain, and set aside.

Heat the olive oil in a large skillet. Add the lemon wedges, capers, olives, and garlic. Reduce the heat and cook very quickly, no more than two minutes. Add the tuna and parsley and stir all the ingredients to combine well and cook evenly. Season with the salt and freshly ground pepper. Add the spiralle to the sauté and toss until they are tangled tastily in the tangy maze of tuna, lemon, olives, and caper sauce.

Mound this labyrinth of flavors into a warmed earthenware bowl and frame with a mosaic border of lemon rounds.

Present this savory offering at a table that conjures up a taverna by the shores of the Aegean. Placemats of rustic Grecian tiles, bold blue and white, need only be illuminated by the softest candlelight to evoke the breezes of the wine-dark sea.

Each serving contains:
- FIBER: 1.4 GRAMS • CHOLESTEROL: 25.3 MILLIGRAMS
- FAT: 19.8 GRAMS

Baked Ziti
Los Angeles

When glamorous grazers go off their diets, they feast on the delectably indulgent Baked Ziti Los Angeles. The above-the-line flavors of mellow roasted tomatoes, fancy wild mushrooms, and the richly pungent majors Gorgonzola, fontina, and Parmesan give this bankable banquet its Rodeo Drive bravado. Second billing goes to a warm spinach salad studded with pine nuts and spicy focaccia to soak up the juices. An icy cup of amaretto granita for dessert will bring down the house.

Makes Six Servings

8 ripe plum tomatoes, quartered
6 cloves garlic, peeled and thinly sliced
1/3 cup chopped fresh parsley
2 tablespoons chopped fresh oregano, or 2 teaspoons dried
1/4 cup chopped fresh basil leaves, or 1 tablespoon dried
3 bay leaves
1 teaspoon salt
1 teaspoon freshly ground black pepper
1/3 cup balsamic vinegar
1/3 cup olive oil, plus 2 1/4 tablespoons

1/4 cup cognac
1 ounce dried Cremini or morel mushrooms, rinsed
   thoroughly
16 ounces ziti tagliati noodles
1 large onion, finely chopped
1/4 teaspoon red-hot pepper flakes
1 teaspoon dried oregano
1 tablespoon butter
1 tablespoon flour
1 cup milk
salt and freshly ground black pepper to taste
freshly grated nutmeg to taste
4 ounces fontina cheese, grated
4 ounces Gorgonzola cheese, crumbled
1/4 cup freshly grated Parmesan cheese

Preheat the oven to 500 degrees.

Place the tomatoes in a single layer in a shallow baking dish, about nine by twelve inches. Sprinkle with half the garlic, two tablespoons of the parsley, and all of the fresh oregano and basil. Nestle in the three bay leaves. Season with salt and pepper. Drizzle the balsamic vinegar and the one-third cup of olive oil over all.

Roast the tomatoes in the oven for eight minutes, until they are lightly caramelized but still retain their shape. Remove the dish from the oven and set aside to cool.

Lower the oven temperature to 350 degrees.

Bring the cognac to a boil in a small saucepan. Add the dried mushrooms, cover, and remove from the heat. Let the mushrooms soak to rehydrate, about thirty minutes.

In five quarts of water, par-cook the ziti at a rolling boil, about seven minutes. Drain the ziti into a colander and rinse under cold water. Set aside in a large bowl.

When the mushrooms have softened, remove them from the cognac with a slotted spoon. Gently squeeze the flavorful excess liquid from the mushrooms over the saucepan of cognac. Set the cognac aside for later. Cut the mushrooms into quarter-inch slices and set aside.

In a large skillet, over low temperature, heat two tablespoons of olive oil. Sauté the onion, the remaining garlic, the red pepper flakes, and the dried oregano. Cook, stirring, until the onion becomes transparent. Add the mushrooms and continue to cook, stirring often. When the mushrooms are tender, stir in the remaining parsley. Turn up the heat to medium temperature. Add the reserved cognac and cook until most of the alcohol has evaporated. Transfer to a bowl and set aside.

Using the same skillet, melt the butter over a low temperature. Briskly stir in the flour. Cook and stir for three minutes until the flour is thoroughly combined with the butter. Pour the milk into the mixture in a stream, whisking continuously. Simmer to thicken, about two minutes. Add the salt, pepper, and nutmeg to taste. Pour this béchamel sauce over the ziti and toss to coat evenly.

Oil a three-quart casserole or baking dish with a quarter tablespoon of olive oil. Use half the roasted tomatoes to line the bottom of the casserole. Drizzle a bit of the tomatoes' juices on top. Cover the tomatoes with a layer of ziti, again using about half, and then a layer of the mushroom mixture, using all. Add the remaining noodles and top with the fontina and Gorgonzola cheeses. Finally add a crowning layer of roasted tomatoes with their juices and garnish with the grated Parmesan.

Cover the casserole with foil. Bake in the oven for twenty minutes. Remove the foil and continue baking for another fifteen minutes, or until the top is puffed and browned. Let the Baked Ziti Los Angeles cool for about five minutes before cutting into squares and serving.

Give your table a Southern Cal topspin — turquoise napkins, a kiss-me-pink tablecloth, sunset dinnerware, and a dramatic centerpiece of huge blooms (odorless, of course).

Lean Noodle Tip: Substitute water for the cognac. Substitute low-fat milk and low-fat cheeses for the whole varieties.

Each Lean Noodle serving contains:
• FIBER: 2.7 GRAMS • CHOLESTEROL: 41 MILLIGRAMS
• FAT: 28.9 GRAMS

Autumn Orecchiette with Pumpkin and Seasonal Herbs

In Apulia, where the southern Italian countryside looks out over the Adriatic, orecchiette are a specialty of the region. Perfectly nestled in each "little ear" of pasta, the fragrant herbs and mellow pumpkin of this aromatic dish seem to capture the mood of autumn. When pumpkin is at its sweetest, spread your table with saucers of olives and almonds and a platter of fried fennel. Sip a crisp vino bianco to toast the flavors of Italy with your family and friends.

Makes Four Servings

> 1 teaspoon fresh thyme, or 1/4 teaspoon dried
> 1 teaspoon chopped fresh sage, or 1/4 teaspoon ground
> 1 teaspoon chopped fresh marjoram, or 1/4 teaspoon dried
> 1/4 teaspoon salt
> 1/2 teaspoon freshly ground black pepper
> 1 small pumpkin, approximate weight 3 pounds
> 12 ounces orecchiette noodles
> 3 tablespoons olive oil
> 2 cloves garlic, peeled and finely chopped
> 3 tablespoons unseasoned bread crumbs

In a small bowl, combine the thyme, sage, marjoram, salt, and pepper.

Cut the top off the pumpkin. Scoop out all the strings and seeds with a metal spoon. Chop the pumpkin into quarters and slice off all the peel. Cut the pumpkin flesh into cubes about one inch square to yield about two cups of cubes.

Bring an inch and a half of water to a boil in a steamer or large deep pot. Place the pumpkin cubes in a wire basket or metal colander. Dust with half of the herb mixture. Steam the pumpkin, covered, over simmering water until tender, about ten to fifteen minutes.

In a large pot, cook the orecchiette in four quarts of boiling water until al dente, about eight minutes.

While the pumpkin and orecchiette are cooking, warm the oil in a medium, heavy-bottomed skillet over medium-high temperature. Add the garlic and sauté for twenty seconds. Toss in the bread crumbs and the remaining mixed herbs and cook, stirring frequently, until the bread crumbs are a crisp golden brown, about four minutes.

Drain the orecchiette and pour into a large, warmed ceramic bowl. Toss well with the steamed pumpkin. For that special savor of the southern Italian countryside, scatter the herbed bread crumbs over all to garnish.

Welcome to a table laden with autumn's harvest: tiny pumpkins decorating each place setting and a centerpiece brimming with fall fruits ripe for the picking to pluck a favorite and linger together over dessert.

Each serving contains:

• FIBER: 0.9 GRAMS • CHOLESTEROL: 0 MILLIGRAMS
• FAT: 11.6 GRAMS